AMERICAN CITIES

PHOENIX

Jacqueline S. Cotton

LET'S READ AV² BY WEIGL™ ADDED VALUE • AUDIO VISUAL

www.av2books.com

Go to **www.av2books.com**, and enter this book's unique code.

BOOK CODE

A V S 8 8 7 3 2

AV^2 by Weigl brings you media enhanced books that support active learning.

AV^2 provides enriched content that supplements and complements this book. Weigl's AV^2 books strive to create inspired learning and engage young minds in a total learning experience.

Your AV^2 Media Enhanced books come alive with...

Audio
Listen to sections of the book read aloud.

Video
Watch informative video clips.

Embedded Weblinks
Gain additional information for research.

Try This!
Complete activities and hands-on experiments.

Key Words
Study vocabulary, and complete a matching word activity.

Quizzes
Test your knowledge.

Slide Show
View images and captions, and prepare a presentation.

... and much, much more!

Published by AV^2 by Weigl
350 5th Avenue, 59th Floor New York, NY 10118
Website: www.av2books.com

Library of Congress Cataloging-in-Publication Data

Names: Cotton, Jacqueline S., author.
Title: Phoenix / Jacqueline S. Cotton.
Description: New York, NY : AV2 by Weigl, [2018] | Series: American cities | Audience: Grades K-3.
Identifiers: LCCN 2018048664 (print) | LCCN 2018049045 (ebook) | ISBN 9781489694652 (Multi User ebook) | ISBN 9781489694751 (Single User ebook) | ISBN 9781489694638 (hardcover : alk. paper) | ISBN 9781489694645 (softcover)
Subjects: LCSH: Phoenix (Ariz.)--Juvenile literature.
Classification: LCC F819.P57 (ebook) | LCC F819.P57 C68 2018 (print) | DDC 979.1/73--dc23
LC record available at https://lccn.loc.gov/2018048664

Printed in the United States of America in Brainerd, Minnesota
1 2 3 4 5 6 7 8 9 0 22 21 20 19 18

112018
051118

Project Coordinator: Heather Kissock Designer: Ana María Vidal

Weigl acknowledges Getty Images, Alamy, Shutterstock, and iStock as the primary image suppliers for this title.

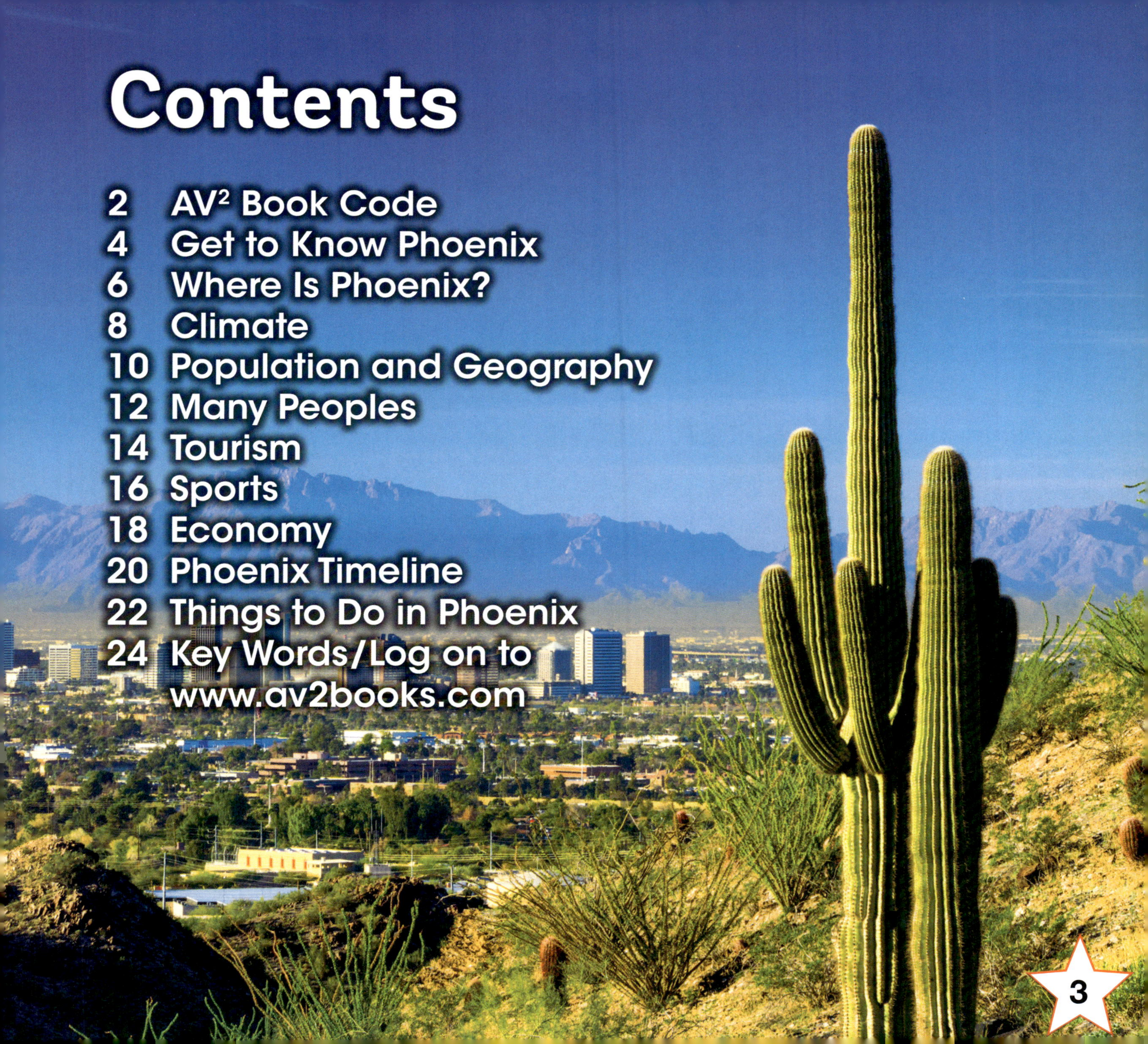

Contents

Get to Know Phoenix

Phoenix is the largest city in the state of Arizona. It is also the state capital. The city was built in a valley. It is known for its sunny days. This is why Phoenix's nickname is "Valley of the Sun."

Map of Arizona

Where Is Phoenix?

Phoenix is in the southwest part of Arizona. It is about 113 miles northwest of Tucson, Arizona's second largest city. You can get to Tucson from Phoenix by driving on the I-10 highway.

There are many other exciting places to visit in Arizona. You can use a road map to plan a trip. Which roads could you take from Phoenix to get to these other places? How long might it take you to get to each place?

TRAVELING ARIZONA
Phoenix to Grand Canyon National Park 224 miles
Phoenix to Alamo Lake State Park 135 miles
Phoenix to Montezuma Castle National Monument 93 miles
Phoenix to Tombstone 184 miles

Climate

Summers in Phoenix are dry and hot. The temperature can rise above 100 degrees Fahrenheit. Monsoons are common. These storms bring dust, wind, and heavy rain.

In the winter, the weather in Phoenix is mild and warm. Many people visit Phoenix during this time of year.

Phoenix gets about **3,800 hours** of sunshine **every year**.

CHASE
WELLS FARGO
ERNST & YOUNG

Population and Geography

Almost 1.6 million people live in Phoenix. This makes Phoenix the fifth largest city in the United States. It is the only state capital with a population of more than 1 million people.

Phoenix is found in the northeast part of the Sonoran Desert. Mountains rise around the city. The Superstition Mountains are east of the city. The White Tank Mountains lie to the west.

Many Peoples

Aboriginal Peoples were the first people to live in the Phoenix area. The U.S. Army built a fort there many years later.

In 1867, a man named Jack Swilling started a settlement in the area. Twenty years later, a railroad was built nearby. People from around the world began to move to Phoenix. Today, people from many different places call the city home.

When Phoenix **first** became a **town**, it was only **1 mile long** and **1/2 mile wide**.

Tourism

Visitors to Phoenix often plan a trip to SEA LIFE Arizona. This aquarium is home to more than 5,000 animals. People can walk through a 360-degree tunnel and watch the animals swim around them.

The Heard Museum is another popular place to go in Phoenix. Here, people can learn more about Native American art and culture.

The **Heard Museum** has more than **40,000 Native American** items on display.

Sports

Phoenix is home to five major sports teams. Its football team, the Cardinals, was founded in 1898. It is the oldest team still playing in the National Football League.

The Diamondbacks play Major League Baseball. The Coyotes play hockey. The men's basketball team is called the Suns. The women's team is called the Mercury.

CARDINALS
13
41

Economy

Tourism is big business in Phoenix. Millions of people visit the city each year. They stay in hotels, eat at restaurants, tour attractions, and buy souvenirs.

Phoenix's Sky Harbor International Airport is one of the busiest airports in the United States. More than 40 million people travel through the airport every year.

In **2016**, tourism brought about **$6 billion** to the city of Phoenix.

Phoenix Timeline

10,000 years ago
Aboriginal Peoples live in the Phoenix area.

1865
U.S. soldiers build Fort McDowell near what is now Phoenix.

1881
Phoenix becomes a city.

1912
Phoenix becomes the capital of Arizona.

1928
Construction begins on Sky Harbor Airport.

1929
The Heard Museum opens.

1990
In June, Phoenix's temperature reaches a record high of 122 degrees.

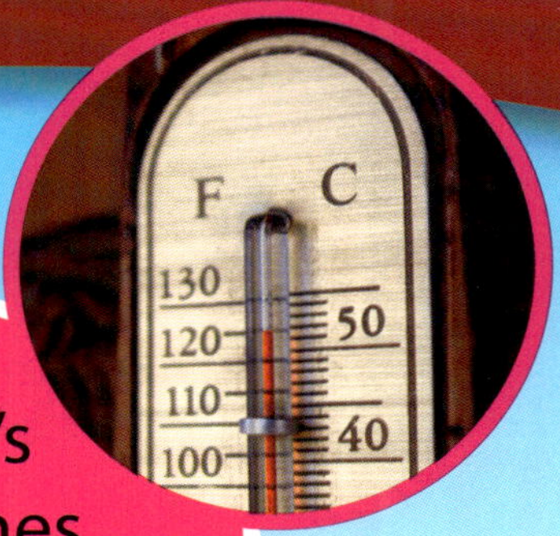

2017
Phoenix is named one of the fastest-growing cities in the United States.

Things to Do in Phoenix

Desert Botanical Garden
About 50,000 desert plants grow in this garden. Visitors can see all of them by walking along five different trails.

Phoenix Zoo
With more than 3,000 animals, the Phoenix Zoo is a popular place to visit. The zoo is home to several rare animals, including the spectacled bear.

Camelback Mountain
This mountain rises 2,704 feet above sea level. Two hiking trails lead to its peak.

Musical Instrument Museum
More than 6,800 musical instruments from about 200 countries are found in this museum.

Arizona Science Center
The Arizona Science Center offers hands-on exhibits and a theater with a five-story-high movie screen.

KEY WORDS

Research has shown that as much as 65 percent of all written material published in English is made up of 300 words. These 300 words cannot be taught using pictures or learned by sounding them out. They must be recognized by sight. This book contains 106 common sight words to help young readers improve their reading fluency and comprehension. This book also teaches young readers several important content words, such as proper nouns. These words are paired with pictures to aid in learning and improve understanding.

Page	Sight Words First Appearance
4	get, know, to
5	a, also, city, days, for, in, is, it, its, of, state, the, this, was, why
7	about, are, by, can, could, each, from, how, long, many, might, miles, on, other, part, places, second, take, there, these, use, where, which, you
8	above, and, every, people, time, year
11	almost, around, found, live, makes, more, mountains, only, than, with
12	began, call, different, first, home, later, man, move, named, started, were, when, world
15	animals, another, go, has, here, learn, often, them, through, walk, watch
16	men, play, still
19	big, eat, one, they
20	near, now, what
21	begins, high, opens
22	all, along, do, grow, plants, see, things
23	feet, hands, story, two

Page	Content Words First Appearance
4	Phoenix
5	Arizona, capital, nickname, Sun, valley
7	highway, road map, trip, Tucson
8	climate, degrees, dust, hours, monsoons, rain, storms, summers, sunshine, temperature, weather, wind, winter
11	geography, population, Sonoran Desert, Superstition Mountains, United States, White Tank Mountains
12	Aboriginal Peoples, area, fort, Jack Swilling, railroad, settlement, town, U.S. Army
15	aquarium, art, culture, display, Heard Museum, items, SEA LIFE Arizona, tourism, tunnel, visitors
16	Cardinals, Coyotes, Diamondbacks, hockey, Major League Baseball, National Football League, Mercury, sports, Suns, teams
19	attractions, business, economy, hotels, restaurants, Sky Harbor International Airport, souvenirs
20	Fort McDowell, soldiers, timeline
21	construction, June
22	Desert Botanical Garden, Phoenix Zoo, spectacled bear, trails
23	Arizona Science Center, Camelback Mountain, countries, exhibits, Musical Instrument Museum, peak, screen, sea level, theater, trails

Check out www.av2books.com for activities, videos, audio clips, and more!

1. **Go to www.av2books.com.**
2. **Enter book code.** **AVS88732**
3. **Fuel your imagination online!**

www.av2books.com